Original title:
Tides of the Ocean's Soul

Copyright © 2025 Creative Arts Management OÜ
All rights reserved.

Author: Miriam Kensington
ISBN HARDBACK: 978-1-80587-274-0
ISBN PAPERBACK: 978-1-80587-744-8

Captured in a Seafoam Whisper

A jellyfish wearing a party hat,
Danced all night with a curious cat.
The waves told secrets in bubbles of cheer,
While seahorses laughed, 'Come join us, dear!'

Starfish played cards on a sandy shore,
Said, 'I'm not good at math, I just want more!'
A crab in a tux tried to cut in line,
But slipped on a conch, said, 'Guess I'm just fine!'

The octopus painted with colors so bright,
Inky spaghetti was quite the delight.
They twirled and jiggled with no sign of care,
While a clam chipped in, 'Do you think I can wear?'

As dolphins sang songs with a splashy twist,
They made waves of laughter; we couldn't resist.
So here's to the sea, with its fun-loving crew,
Where laughter floats high, and dreams come true!

Beneath the Surface

Down below where crabs dance tight,
Clams compose their late-night write.
Seaweed sways in a silly jig,
While fish debate who's best in fig.

An octopus plays hide and seek,
While shells gossip, all quite unique.
Starfish watch with a wink and grin,
As bubbles rise and the fun begins.

Whispers Rise

In the depths, the sea cucumbers sigh,
While seals tell jokes and dolphins fly.
A wise old turtle drops his truth,
Life's a laugh beneath the blue youth.

Gulls squawk loudly, making a scene,
While crabs engage in their lively routine.
They argue over treasures so bright,
"Who stole my shells?"—a quirky sight.

Salt and Serenity in the Abyss

Where the sea foam tickles the shore,
A jellyfish drifts, what a bore!
It stings with flair, but just for fun,
As laughter bubbles, all in the sun.

Clownfish joke, "I'm the star, you see,"
While anemones sway, as wild as can be.
Salted air brings giggles alive,
In harmony, all creatures thrive.

Motion of the Darkened Depths

In shadowed depths, the eels wiggle,
Trying hard not to giggle.
Crabs paint themselves in bright, bold hues,
Wishing for brushes, they can't refuse.

The squids juggle seashells with grace,
Making all fishes join in the race.
Even the deepest laughs can be bright,
In the dark where no sun shines light.

Reflections of a Celestial Tide

Under the moon, goldfish shine,
While otters toast with sweet brine.
Laughter floats on the rippling wave,
In friendships deep, the ocean's brave.

The otters race with such delight,
Splashing around 'til the morn's first light.
They hoot and holler with silly cheers,
Washing away all the worries and fears.

Woven from Salt and Sunlight

The seaweed's waltz in twisted glee,
Caught a crab who sipped her tea.
With every wave, a laugh did swell,
As starfish plotted jokes to tell.

A dolphin danced, its jumps so spry,
While seagulls chirp, 'Oh me, oh my!'
A splash of fun, the beach was bold,
With sandy tales of laughter told.

Afloat on the Surface of Sentiments

A rubber duck on a wild ride,
Made friends with waves, none could abide.
With giggles echoing in the spray,
It quacked about its splashing play.

A jellyfish joined the circus show,
With tentacle tricks that stole the glow.
While fish threw confetti from the reef,
This floating party, beyond belief!

Spirits of the Shoreline

Two crabs sat plotting a great heist,
Stealing shells, they thought it nice.
With each small plan, they danced with grace,
Until sand tickled, showing their face.

Along came a whale, a singing star,
Cracking jokes to lift the bizarre.
The shoreline chuckled, all in delight,
As waves rolled in to join the night.

Vessels of Vain Dreams

A ship of dreams with sails of sighs,
Set out to find the silly skies.
Its captain wore a hat of cheese,
With a compass that pointed toward the breeze.

The crew was made of playful sprites,
Who danced even when the sea ignites.
They laughed at storms, said, 'What a show!'
While fishy friends joined in the flow.

Beneath the Cresting Silence

The waves tell jokes, but they can't laugh,
They're rolling in with a bubbly gaff.
The seagulls squawk their comic refrain,
As crabs tap dance in their sandy lane.

A fish flipped out, gave quite a stare,
Wiggled and flopped, what a wild affair!
With a splash it vanished, as if to flee,
Leaving behind just a bemused sea.

Where the Wild Waters Roar

The river gurgles, it tickles and teases,
Flowing past rocks, where humor never ceases.
A duck floats by, quacking with cheer,
Wearing a crown made of kelp—oh dear!

Fish joke in bubbles, in slapstick delight,
Thrashing about in an underwater fight.
A starfish waved, while telling a pun,
But got distracted by a ray of sun.

An Offering to the Great Expanse

Upon the shore, a crab offered his shell,
As a gift to the sea, it rang like a bell.
"Take my home! It's quite a delight,
Just watch out for waves; they'll give you a fright!"

The sand sang softly, with grains taking flight,
While gulls held court, in midair flight.
"Life's a beach!" they cawed, in humorous jest,
As the tide pulled back, giving all a rest.

The Horizon's Lament at Dusk

As day bids adieu, the sun takes a dive,
While jellyfish dance, feeling quite alive.
A crab thinks of joining, but then he forgot,
His dance moves are silly, awkward at best shot.

The stars peek down, with a giggle and wink,
While fish swarm about, in the deep blue drink.
"Let's party!" they shout, in the shimmering wave,
With laughter that echoes, mischief they crave.

Soul-stirred by the Depths

Bubbles rise like giggles bright,
Fish wear hats, oh what a sight!
Coral reefs twist and twirl,
An octopus does a funny whirl.

Seashells gossip, secrets share,
While dolphins dance without a care.
Crabs in tuxedos pick a fight,
Waving claws with all their might.

The starfish tells a clumsy joke,
As seaweed sways and nearly chokes.
A whale sneezes, what a sound!
The ocean laughs, spins 'round and 'round.

Odes to the Endless Blue

Mermaids sing with silly rhyme,
Their hair entangled all the time.
A jellyfish floats by with flair,
Wearing sunglasses, quite the pair!

Fish prank each other at the reef,
One wears seaweed like a brief.
A seagull squawks, 'Who dropped that pie?'
The ocean chuckles, oh my, oh my!

Barnacles sport tiny hats,
Inviting friends for coastal chats.
Octopi juggle shells and flounder,
The depths of blue, oh such a wonder!

The Cessation of Storms

The waves now pause, they take a break,
A crab spreads tales with a big cake.
The seagulls play hide and seek,
Wave after wave, it's all quite chic.

The squall's away, the sun comes out,
Fish gossip freely, there's no doubt.
A snail slides in, grandpa on land,
Saying, 'In the calm, we make grand plans!'

The octopus knits with seaweed thread,
Making sweaters for friends, it's said.
In lazy swirls, the sky turns blue,
The sea's a party, look at that view!

Luminous Murmurs in the Abyss

Glowworms giggle in the night,
Their lanterns flashing, oh what a sight!
The deep is filled with muffled cheer,
As anglerfish draw near, oh dear!

Whales whisper secrets, deeply shy,
While squids squirt ink and say goodbye.
A clownfish jokes with all its might,
Dancing in waters, what a delight!

The moonlit waves play peek-a-boo,
While creatures paint the ocean blue.
The deep sea's humor makes us grin,
A cocoon of laughter, round and round we spin.

Embracing the Water's Veil

Splashing around in my rubber raft,
I drift and I giggle, can't help but laugh.
Fish are my neighbors, they swim with glee,
I swear they do wave back; it's not just me.

Seagulls are know-it-alls, squawking loud,
Chasing my sandwich, they're quite the crowd.
I shout, 'Hey, buddy! That's my lunch!'
They dive like ninjas, what a weird hunch!

I tried to swim, but ended up splashing,
With every wave, I just kept crashing.
The ocean's a joker, it's clear to see,
My buoyant ballet is pure comedy!

As waves roll in with a cheeky grin,
They laugh at my flops, encourage my spin.
I'm part of their jokes—out here in the blue,
A clumsy performer in their grand review!

A Wanderer's Song amid the Waves

With flip-flops squeaking on the hot sand,
I prance like a crab that can barely stand.
Sandy snacks seem to fly from my hand,
All the beach life must think I'm unplanned!

The whispers of waves tease my sunbaked skin,
Come join the splash fest, they chime, "Jump in!"
But upon my arrival, I trip, then I flop,
Making quite the spectacle, a belly flop pop!

The mermaids are laughing, oh what a sight,
As I flounder about, quite full of fright.
They flip their tails and twinkle their eyes,
While I swim like a penguin in desperate tries!

Sunburned and giggly, I lose the race,
The waves tease me back, keeping up the chase.
Each splash writes a story, both silly and bright,
A wanderer's journey in pure delight!

The Soul's Voyage Through Brine

A vessel of laughter, afloat in the sea,
My captain's a cat, he's sailing with glee.
Under the stars—or just chips and dip,
With every soft wave, my dreams start to flip.

The jellyfish jiggle, like disco balls bright,
And sea cucumbers dance with sheer delight.
I tried to keep up—but alas, I fell down,
As crabs played the banjo, clad in the crown!

Oh, what a ruckus, this salty life scene,
With octopus friends, no one's ever mean.
They serve up the laughs, as I paddle my fate,
In an inflatable boat—oh, please don't deflate!

The ocean is quirky, a splashy ballet,
With dolphins that sum up my colorful day.
Each bubble's a whisper of joy on the breeze,
Sailing life's waters, we're all just at ease!

Shores Adrift in Time

Beneath the sun, where the seagulls dive,
I've lost my flip-flops, but hey, I'm alive!
The waves tell stories of long-lost socks,
In my sandy kingdom, I'm king of the rocks.

A crab in a tuxedo waltzes by me,
Offering compliments, oh, what a spree!
I laugh at the thought of my beach-perfect strut,
While sneezing at sand—oh boy, that's a glut!

The shells chime a tune of the foolish and free,
As I dance with the stars, a true sight to see.
Oh, the sunset wraps tales of laughter and sway,
At shores adrift, all worries give way.

Each wave carries choices I've made with a grin,
As mermaids hold secrets, how funny we swim!
Time's but a trickster, oh silly and bright,
In the great ocean's heart, we float through the night!

Moonlit Caress

Under the moon, the waves do sway,
Dancing like fish in a cabaret.
Seagulls squawk in their best croon,
While crabs join in with a cheeky tune.

The stars giggle, they wink and beam,
As jellyfish float like a wild dream.
With each splash, the shore does grin,
For night's silly games to begin.

Sandcastles tumble like a weak joke,
While the ocean teases with a gentle poke.
Giggles echo through salty breeze,
As fish start to shimmy, oh what a tease!

So raise a shell to the silly scene,
Where waves keep dancing, and all is seen.
With laughter and joy in every roll,
We find the humor in the ocean's soul.

Serenade of the Swell

The swell sings sweet, in a wink and nod,
Dolphins spin with a flip and plod.
They joke with the skies, a grand ballet,
As fish tell tales in a bubbly display.

Crabs wear shades, they stroll with pride,
While seaweed dances, it sways with the tide.
The rocks chuckle, their faces worn,
As conch shells laugh at the ships that are torn.

"Why'd the octopus cross the sea?"
To get to the other tide, you see!
Each wave a punchline, each splash a cheer,
Giggling creatures, holding back tears.

So let's raise a toast to the ocean's wit,
For laughter is found in every bit.
With foam on the shore, and mirth in the swell,
The sea keeps secrets, oh, do tell!

Journeys on the Water's Edge

On the sandy shore, where rubber ducks roam,
Starfish wear hats, like they're at home.
A crab in a hurry, oh what a sight,
Chasing a wave, with all of its might.

Seashells gossip with laughter and cheer,
Sharing their stories for all who can hear.
As kids dig deep for treasure beneath,
Little do they know, it's just a false sheath.

The pelican's swoop, a comical flop,
Landing in seaweed, he gives a plop!
With sand in his beak, and fish in a trance,
He shuffles away, not quite in advance.

So let's wander and wander, by the bright sea's edge,
With giggles and chuckles, a playful pledge.
Each journey a comedy, each wave a jest,
With laughter and joy, the ocean's best!

Beneath the Surface's Veil

Bubbles rise up, they wiggle and pop,
A fish in a bowtie just can't stop.
With gills all a-flutter, he joins the show,
"Why wear fins when I can wear a bow?"

The sea cucumber giggles, it's quite the catch,
Tell me your secrets, I'll raise you a batch!
The octopus winks, says, "Give me a hand!"
And all of his arms come together, so grand.

Under the waves, it's a carnival spree,
With laughter and joy as wild as can be.
The sea floor's alive with a whimsical spin,
Where each fish has a tale, and grins from within.

So join in the fun, take a dive if you dare,
For beneath the surface, there's humor to share.
With giggles and laughter in bubbles that swell,
The ocean's a circus, it's ringing the bell!

Lullabies of Nereus

In the deep, fish wear pajamas,
Starfish dance, like out-of-work dramas.
Squids play cards, a slippery game,
While crabs gossip about who's to blame.

Jellyfish bounce, just floating around,
With seaweed wigs, they twirl, quite profound.
A whale sings off-key, yet all stay near,
Laughing so hard, they forget their fear.

Where the Deep Meets the Sky

Seagulls shout, 'Yo! We want your fries!'
While dolphins plot their next big surprise.
Clouds throw shade, just chilling on high,
As fish below ponder the art of the fry.

Octopus chefs serve meals with flair,
But of course, they can never find a spare.
Surfboards sigh as waves go to play,
'Take it easy, man; it's a lazy day!'

Sun-kissed Ripples

Crabs wearing sunscreen hug the shore,
While clam-shells hold a beach party galore.
A sun-kissed snail moves at a crawl,
Saying, 'Slow and steady wins it for all!'

The seaweed swings as if in a trance,
A fishy ballet, they leap, then prance.
Sandcastles tremble, oh what a sight,
As waves giggle, and take a big bite!

Shells of Lost Whispers

Secrets hide deep in each polished shell,
Whispers of fish who in bubbles dwell.
A clam once dreamed of a trip to the moon,
But woke up to find it'd been chewing on June!

Crabs debate fashion; who wore it best?
With pearls in their pockets, they surely are blessed.
Anemones giggle, don't take it too hard,
In this watery circus, we're all the backyard.

Navigator of the Heart's Waters

With a compass made of jelly,\nI sail through dreams so sweet,\nNavigating through the guacamole,\nLaughing as the waves hit my feet.\n\nMy ship is made of pizza crust,\nEach slice a daring delight,\nSwabbing decks with sticky buns,\nEven the seagulls think I'm right!\n\nBumpy rides on chocolate waves,\nI dance like no one can see,\nSwirling like a merry fish,\nMy heart's the captain, oh me!\n\nWhen storms of broccoli approach,\nI steer clear, it's quite the joke,\nWith laughter ringing through the night,\nI'll row that boat, I'll make it float!

In the Embrace of the Sea's Breath

Crabs doing the cha-cha on the shore,\nAs the surf serenades their groove,\nA clam's a DJ, spinning seashell beats,\nIn the ocean's waltz, we move.\n\nSeagulls squawk a karaoke tune,\nWhile dolphins join in the fun,\nThe sand's our dance floor, so smooth and bright,\nLaughter echoes, we're never done!\n\nSalty breeze brings whispers of dreams,\nOctopus serving up tall tales,\nWith zestful pals, we plot our pranks,\nIn this watery world, joy prevails!\n\nBut watch out for the jellyfish,\nThey think they're the life of the bash,\nWith all their wobbly, wiggly moves,\nThey're just here to ruin the splash!

The Vastness Beneath

In the depths, where the fishes joke,\nA whale told a tale, quite a poke,\nWith bubbles and giggles, they passed the time,\nThe ocean's laughter is simply sublime.\n\nSquids wearing hats, what a sight to see,\nSwirling like stars in a new comedy,\nI snorkel through puns that make me grin,\nAmidst the corals, let the fun begin!\n\nAnemones giggle as I swim by,\n"Don't tickle us, or you'll make us cry!"\nFish have a laugh, they chat in streams,\nIn this watery realm, it's all about dreams.\n\nWhen crabs try to dance but just trip and crawl,\nTheir sideways antics, we're having a ball,\nSo dive deep, my friend, join in the spree,\nIn the vastness below, there's always glee!

Vanishing Echoes of Salt and Spray

In the foamy waves, a tale was spun,\nA sea sponge donned a pirate's hat for fun,\nWith squishy laughter echoing loud,\nHe raised a toast to the bubbly crowd!\n\nStarfish juggling sea cucumbers,\nMermaids sing songs with a twist,\nA kraken plays cards, quite the conniver,\nWhile jellyfish glow in an electric mist.\n\n"Oh, watch out for the clam!" someone shouts,\n"She's got a secret, no doubts!"\nBut in this frolicsome, salty ball,\nMemories of laughter always enthrall.\n\nSo let's paint the waves with colors so bright,\nAs the seagulls laugh with sheer delight,\nTogether we'll dance on the spray's sweet breath,\nIn this ocean of joy, there's no room for death!

Moonlit Serenades on the Water

Under the moon's cheeky grin,
Fish jump high as if to win.
Crabs are dancing, crabs are free,
What a sight, a jubilee!

Seagulls squawk, a comedic show,
Stealing snacks while on the go.
Waves crash like a laughing crowd,
Silly whispers, none too loud!

Bubbles rise, they pop and play,
Casting magic in their spray.
Frogs croak tunes in perfect time,
Each note a giggle, so sublime!

Oh, the ocean's jolly spree,
Who knew blue could laugh with glee?
Ride the wave, but mind the splash,
A splashy joke, a water bash!

Salted Dreams and Distant Shores

Seagulls snicker, what a sight,
Chasing boats with all their might.
Shells are giggling on the sand,
Wishing fate would make them grand!

Starfish lounge like they're on break,
Living life for fun's sweet sake.
Sandcastles with a silly twist,
Dodge the tide, you can't resist!

A crab in shades, what a fashion!
Swims so smooth, a funny passion.
Mermaids laugh, they lost their comb,
Hiding treasures far from home!

Distant shores call out for cheers,
Waves tell tales of goofy years.
Dreams are salty, slightly sweet,
Life's a dance, don't miss a beat!

Dance of the Endless Horizon

Pelicans dive in comical flair,
Making waves with little care.
The horizon smiles, a cheeky tease,
It plays peek-a-boo with the breeze!

Boats swerve round like swirling kites,
Fishermen giggle, sharing bites.
A dolphin pops, a twist and shout,
In this ocean game, there's no doubt!

Octopus inks a silly doodle,
While jellyfish get caught in a noodle.
Mermaids twirl in a whirl of fun,
Turning sunbeams to a run!

The endless dance goes on and on,
Twirling 'til the early dawn.
With laughter loud, the sea's delight,
Join the jig, it feels so right!

Requiem for the Roiling Sea

Gallant waves in a silly fuss,
Frothy hiccups riding the bus.
Whales compose a jolly tune,
Belting notes beneath the moon!

The sea's a stage, a comical act,
Cranky currents, bound to attract.
Sailors stumble, dodging spray,
Each smirk a star in their ballet!

Barnacles wear hats so bright,
Waving hello with pure delight.
A sea cucumber plans a prank,
In the swirling depths, it's a tank!

So here's to the waves, in jest they roll,
Making merry, that's the goal.
The ocean's heart beats wild and free,
In laughter's wave, we find our glee!

Chasing Shadows on Water

Catch the waves, they wiggle and dance,
Like jellyfish trying to wear pants.
Seagulls giggle, diving for fries,
While crabs play tag, plotting their lies.

A boat floats by, plus a sunburned chap,
Who slips and flips in his sun-hat trap.
The dolphins laugh, flip-flopping in glee,
As we splash about, feeling quite free.

Fish flip-flop under the sun's hot glow,
Planning their heist, their sneaky show.
A snail races by, taking it slow,
While everyone else just seems to throw.

The ocean's a joker, always in jest,
Delivering punchlines, guaranteeing rest.
With laughter and waves, we float along,
Creating our melody, forever strong.

Rippling Memories

Bubbles pop like secrets in the breeze,
As sandcastles lose to the playful squeeze.
A frisbee sails, but lands in a pie,
And we all burst out laughing, oh my, oh my!

Old seagulls squabble, claiming their space,
While I trip over my own shoelace.
Shells whisper stories, giggling in code,
As the tide creeps in, carrying the load.

I find a message in a bottle of glass,
"Help! I'm glad I'm not made of grass!"
The ocean just chuckles, rolling in glee,
With jokes in the foam, for you and for me.

As the sun bids adieu with a sparkly grin,
The stars trade jokes as the night begins.
I wave to the crabs, they nod with delight,
We'll meet in the morning, it feels just right.

Symphony of the Distant Horizon

The sunset plays tunes on the water's face,
As waves strum along, keeping up the pace.
A seagull starts crooning, off-key, but loud,
While the fish join in, luring quite the crowd.

Here comes a walrus with sunglasses on,
He's conducting the waves with a splashy yawn.
Clams tap their shells, keeping time with a beat,
As the ocean orchestra gets on its feet.

A lobster waltzes, with moves so divine,
While starfish clap, feeling just fine.
The jellyfish glow like disco lights,
Making every wave dance under night sights.

As night falls down, the laughter will swell,
With fishy puns that we all know so well.
The sea's concert ends with a bubbly goodnight,
Leaving echoes of laughter, oh what a sight!

Cradled by the Sea

The waves rocked me gently, oh what a plot,
Is that a mermaid, or a very wet cat?
She wiggles and jigs in the seaweed parade,
While clumsy old me gets twirled and delayed.

A crab in a top hat thinks he's so grand,
He tips his shell as we all cheer and stand.
The fish gather 'round for the show of the year,
With laughter that bubbles, oh let's lift a cheer!

A sunken treasure full of old shoes,
That fish play with daily; who knew they'd amuse?
We throw in our wishes, but they come back wet,
Turns out this ocean has items to vet!

As we all float back, giggling with glee,
The ocean gives hugs, as warm as can be.
With humor and joy, nestled in foam,
We find in this laughter, our true happy home.

Melody of the Moonlit Waters

The moon dances on waves with glee,
While fish throw a rave and giggle with me.
They wiggle and jive, a slippery sight,
As crabs form a band, playing all night.

Seagulls join in, with their squawking tunes,
While jellyfish glow like funky balloons.
Each splash and each flip, a comical chase,
Even the shells up and join the race!

The starfish critique, with a wink and a grin,
Saying, "You call that a dance? Try again, fin!"
The laughter bursts forth, it circles the bay,
As waves tease the sand, in this joyous display.

So if you feel low, come join the parade,
Where the waters are bouncy and merrily played.
With moonlight above and fun all around,
You'll find joy where nature's lost and found.

The Heartbeat of the Horizon

The sun yawns big, with a wink in the sky,
As seagulls race clouds, oh my, oh my!
With every splash, the dolphins all cheer,
While boats laugh aloud at the waves they steer.

"Yo ho!" calls the pirate, but his hat flies away,
Chasing the breeze, it runs off to play.
The fish roll their eyes, not missing a wink,
As mermaids giggle and let the waves sink.

The horizon blushes in colors so bright,
While crabs throw a tea party, what a delight!
With scones made of seaweed and tea brewed from brine,

Who knew the ocean could host such a dine?

So if laughter's your quest, come gather around,
Let the rhythm of waves fill the air with sound.
The heartbeat of banter's a thing we all share,
In the laughter of currents where joy's everywhere.

Reflections in the Brine

The water winks back, with a giggle so sly,
As sea turtles crack jokes beneath the bright sky.
"Did you hear about fish who rode on a wave?,"
Said one little clown, feeling way too brave.

They laughed at each splash, with bubbles of fun,
As sea urchins chuckled, hiding in the sun.
"Take a seat on a seashell; it's comfy and neat!"
While octopus jesters drew doodles so sweet.

A crab once declared, "I'm the king of this reef!"
But the fish just rolled over, in disbelief.
"Your royal highness, please stick to the sand!"
As laughter rolled over like waves on the strand.

So come grab a shell, let's party and jive,
With reflections of mirth where the sea comes alive.
In the brine we'll find joy, floating along,
In this comical ballet, we all belong!

Celestial Conversations

Stars flicker gossip, with the moon on the side,
As tides huddle close, in their watery stride.
"Did you hear what the sun said to the sea?"
"Something about sandcastles, oh let's wait and see!"

The clouds overheard, and they started to drift,
In a fluffy debate, oh what a fine gift!
"Do you think the tide can keep secrets so deep?"
While dolphins cavorted, not missing a beat.

"Let's throw a big party!" the ocean did roar,
"Bring your best jokes, we'll laugh 'til we're sore!"
So they all joined in, in a great cosmic jest,
Bringing mirth to the sea, oh, it's simply the best!

So if the sky grins and the waves start to sway,
Join the celestial chatter, don't shy away!
For the humor of waters and stars up above,
Is a dance full of laughter, a swirl of pure love.

Driftwood Chronicles

Once a piece of driftwood lost,
It floated, loving every cost.
With seaweed hats and barnacle shoes,
It laughed at waves, refusing to snooze.

Bobbing up in jellyfish bars,
Telling tales of fishy scars.
It traded jokes with a rogue wave,
Claiming to be a wooden brave.

A crab, with snappy claws, did shout,
"What's your secret? Don't sell out!"
"I just float and soak up sun,"
Said driftwood, always on the run.

So every day's a party ride,
With sea life dancing by its side.
In ocean's heart, such glee was found,
A driftwood legend, joy unbound.

Beneath the Sailor's Sky

The sailor gazes, lost in dreams,
His parrot squawks, or so it seems.
'To find a treasure, one must dive!'
But all he finds is fish that jive.

With every wave, a hiccup's felt,
His compass spins, his plans are dealt.
"X marks the spot!" he shouts in cheer,
Yet finds a crab clutching a beer.

Stars above twinkle like his plans,
Mapping adventures with flailing hands.
The mermaids giggle, splashing around,
While the sailor spins in circles, confound.

In laughter's grip, they sail the night,
Chasing dreams 'neath the moonlight bright.
And though he's lost, he wears a grin,
For fun, not riches, is where he's been.

Waves of Undying Longing

Oh, silly waves that crash and play,
I wish they'd float my cares away.
Instead, they tease with frothy laughs,
   And tickle toes in salty baths.

A love once sought on shifting sand,
A seashell whispered, take my hand.
But each time I reached with hope so bold,
A seagull swooped, my lunch did scold.

   The ocean's heart, a fickle affair,
While jellyfish just swim with flair.
I swim for love, it runs from me,
In ocean's jest, I'm fish, not free.

But who needs love when fun's the game?
I dive, I dip, I dance, I claim.
With every splash, I laugh and sing,
These waves may tease, but joy they bring.

Glistening Horizons

Look out yonder, the shine so bright,
A gull's on a mission: a snack tonight.
With horizons painted gold and blue,
It dreams of sushi, a fishy stew.

The sunbeams sparkle, like disco balls,
While turtles groove, ignoring calls.
"Don't forget your sunscreen!" a whale did say,
As dolphins joined in for a fun ballet.

But what's that on the horizon's end?
A beach ball lost, will it transcend?
It bobbles near the sandy shore,
A comedic sight, we can't ignore.

So let's rejoice beneath this sky,
With laughter echoing, let worries fly.
For every wave that rolls on through,
Brings glistening giggles, old and new.

Sandcastles of Ephemeral Thoughts

Building castles made of sand,
My dreams wash away by a wave's hand.
Seagulls laugh at my lofty plans,
While I pretend to be a king with lands.

Buckets full of hope and might,
I sculpt my visions, yet they take flight.
The tide rolls in, I panic and flee,
My royal throne, now a crab's marquee!

As shells become my treasured gold,
I trade my crown for stories bold.
Beneath the sun, I dance and tumble,
While my sandy kingdom starts to crumble.

Yet joy is found in such a mess,
As waves come in, who needs success?
For laughter lives where dreams go gray,
In castles crumbly, we'll find our play.

Celestial Navigation of the Mind

Starfish drift with lazy ease,
While I'm lost among the seas.
My thoughts like boats set sail at night,
But bump the shore, what a sight!

With a map of squiggles and laughs,
I seek the stars like a fisherman's haffs.
But the constellations have other plans,
Go fish, they say, my catch is bland!

Navigating chaos, I find delight,
As my mental compass spins with fright.
Each thought a wave, a splash of fun,
Oh, why can't navigation be done?

So here I sail, with joy in tow,
Lost in the cosmos, but so aglow.
In the sea of thoughts, I'll ride the tide,
With laughter as my trusty guide.

The Sea's Silent Soliloquy

Oh, the sea speaks in whispers low,
Crabs hold court, in their spiky show.
With barnacles as their trusty mates,
They tell tall tales of their types of fates.

A fish in a bowler hat swims by,
With dreams of being a starfish fly.
While jellyfish float with dazzling grace,
They laugh at humans in their busy race.

The waves roll in with giggles and glee,
As I listen; it's just me and the sea.
Echoes of laughter, both near and far,
In this watery theater, I'm a bizarre star.

So I sit and ponder with a grin,
This oceanic jest, where life's a win.
Each splash a joke, each wave a tease,
In the sea's silent play, my mind's at ease.

Journeys Through the Blue Abyss

Packing my dreams in a clammy shell,
Off to explore where the sea creatures dwell.
With a snorkel and mask, I'm ready to dive,
Searching for giggles where fish come alive.

Squid with wigs and octopuses twirling,
Dance beneath the waves, oh so swirling.
In the deep blue, humor flows like the tide,
As clownfish bubble, and dolphins slide!

A treasure map that leads nowhere at all,
Just where the laughing sea cucumbers crawl.
I chase them around, what a tangled spree,
In this ridiculous, watery jubilee!

So here's to journeys in the ocean's embrace,
Where laughter bubbles up, what a silly place!
Let's ride the waves and let our hearts race,
In the blue abyss, we've found our space.

A Canvas of Blue Horizons

In a place where sea gulls squawk,
The fish dance, not a care to mock.
A crab in shades of summer's blush,
Waves whisper, 'Hurry, it's time to rush!'

With buckets and shovels, kids dream wide,
Building castles with shells as their guide.
But the tide comes in with a sneaky grin,
Crashing their dreams like a playful din.

Sandcastles fall with a flourish and spray,
While laughing seashells join in the play.
Jumping up high, like seabirds take flight,
The ocean's giggles echo in the night.

So grab a float and ride the swell,
In this watery world where sea creatures dwell.
With laughter and splashes, the day feels grand,
A canvas of joy on the sun-kissed sand.

Heartstrings of the Ocean

The fish have a party, the jellyfish sway,
While crabs shuck and jive in the ocean's ballet.
A dolphin jokes, flipping, then takes a bow,
With seaweed confetti, they're all here now.

Octopus plays the drums with great flair,
While starfish high-fives in the salty air.
The anchor's not heavy, it's just playing shy,
As mermaids twirl, laughing with a sigh.

But watch that sea cucumber, he's got some moves,
With a shimmy and shake, he grooves and improves.
The waves are our music, a splashy refrain,
We dance with the currents, forget all our pain.

In the depths of the blue where the sun beams glow,
Each creature's a friend, together they flow.
With heartstrings entwined, we sing out our tune,
In this underwater world, beneath the moon.

The Splendor of Untamed Waves

Oh the waves have a mind of their own,
With foamy gigs and splashes that shone.
Like giddy children on a rainy day,
They tumble and chatter, come out to play.

A seal in sunglasses floats by with ease,
Bobbing along, teasing the sea breeze.
While barnacles gossip about local lore,
'Did you see that whale? He opened the door!'

The current is quirky, all twists and turns,
As shoals of fish dance, the ocean churns.
Spray of water like confetti confides,
In this grand celebration, nature provides.

So let's grab our surfboards, let laughter abound,
Catch the wild waves, let joy be unwound.
For in every splash, there's a story to share,
The fun of the ocean, a party laid bare.

Where Dusk Meets the Sea

As the sun waves goodbye, the moon takes its stand,
Starfish gather 'round, making a band.
With phosphorescent lights, they twinkle just right,
Creating a show, dancing into the night.

The seagulls are yawning, perched up on high,
Counting the stars as they drift in the sky.
A whale's serenade echoes through the waves,
While fish join in chorus, in bubbly enclaves.

As crabs start a limbo, all nimble and spry,
The dolphins dive deep, leaping through the sky.
The currents are humming a catchy old tune,
And jellyfish float by, like balloons in the moon.

So let loose your worries and dance with the tide,
In this silly soirée, where laughter's a guide.
At the edge of the dusk, where the sea kisses land,
Funny friends gather, holding a sea-shell band.

Waves Whispering Secrets

Waves come in, with giggles and glee,
They've got jokes only fish can see.
A crab tells tales of a glorious fight,
While dolphins make splashy puns in the night.

Seagulls swoop down, they squawk and they squabble,
Dropping their snacks, oh what a trouble!
Each roll of the sea, a joke to unfold,
In the salty dance, stories are told.

With foam on their lips, and shells as their stage,
The ocean's a clown, turning youth into age.
Whispers abound in this watery place,
Laughter erupts like a bubbly embrace.

So listen closely, as the waves laugh and cheer,
The ocean's humor is crystal clear.
In ripples and splashes, the fun won't cease,
For every big wave brings a small piece of peace.

Currents of Eternal Change

The current's a prankster, always in motion,
Whipping up whirlpools like a wild ocean.
It shifts like a dancer, never stands still,
Plotting new routes with its playful thrill.

Fish tell tall tales of currents that tickle,
With each sudden twist, they giggle and giggle.
"Where are we swimming?" they ask in dismay,
"Every direction feels a bit like a play!"

Even the mermaids chuckle and grin,
As the waves pull them, laughing within.
"Let's swim upside down, and see who outplays,
The currents of life in their silly displays!"

So the lesson is clear, as the waters flow free,
Embrace the absurd, let your heart be a spree.
Dance with the winds, in this bubbly expanse,
For change may be funny if given a chance.

The Heartbeat of the Deep

Beneath the waves, there's a heart that beats,
A rhythmic thumping where the oddity greets.
It pulses with laughter, deep down in a cave,
Where octopuses play the finest charade.

Each wave's a giggle, each swell brings a jest,
The creatures are rebels, never at rest.
Anemones dance, with a shake of their hips,
Sardines swarm in for a round of quick flips.

The deep blue sings of whimsical tunes,
With jellyfish jamming beneath silver moons.
And all of the sea critters join in the fun,
Casting their shadows, a humorous run.

So listen for laughter, beneath the grand blue,
For the heartbeat of ocean whispers "Come too!"
Join in the joy, as the waters all play,
Finding delight in each silly display.

Echoes in the Blue Abyss

In the depths where the light barely shines,
Echoes of chuckles weave through the lines.
"Is that a whale or a big rubber duck?"
The questions arise, who would've guessed luck?

Silly sea turtles in dramatic slow mo,
Pose for a selfie, as if they know.
"Look at us swim," they proudly declare,
"In this echoing chamber, we haven't a care!"

And deep in the darkness, the clams start to hum,
Balancing pearls like they're part of a drum.
Their laughter's a treasure, a sound for the brave,
In the blue abyss, where silliness waves.

So if you are swimming where echoes ignite,
Remember the laughter that plays in the night.
For beneath the blue skies, and the shimmering sea,
There's humor aplenty, just waiting for thee.

Currents of Forgotten Dreams

The fish wear top hats, oh what a sight,
As they dance around, in the pale moonlight.
A crab tells a joke, but it's a bit crusty,
The seaweed just giggles, all green and dusty.

Seashells play poker on a sandy shore,
Betting their pearls, while the waves roar.
A dolphin swims by, with a grin so wide,
Says, "If you lose, blame the tide!"

The starfish cheer loud, with five little claps,
While turtles take naps, in their cozy laps.
Old octopus jokes, they twist and they bend,
Mixing mischief with humor, they'll never end.

With each splash and ripple, a story unfolds,
The ocean whispers secrets, both young and old.
So come laugh with the fish, and splash all around,
In this waterlogged circus where joy can be found.

Echoes Beneath the Waves

Bubbles float up with a giggle and pop,
While sea cucumbers practice their hop.
A bottle-nosed dolphin, so smart and so sly,
Teases a sea turtle that's passing it by.

Giant clams sing songs, baritone and sweet,
While crabs breakdance down on the sea-stone street.
A seahorse spins tales of romance and fun,
Promised sweet hugs when the day is done.

The jellyfish jitter in a wobbly waltz,
A sea urchin grumbles, "Oh what are the faults?"
While corals make crowns, all regal and bright,
Casting corny puns into the night.

In the underwater disco, they wiggle and sway,
With bubbles and laughter, we dance and we play.
Echoes of joy rise with each gentle wave,
The ocean's a jester, it's silly and brave.

Secrets in the Sand

A crab burrows down, hides treasures galore,
But he's lost his keys, oh what a bore!
Seashells are winking, with secrets to share,
Of pirates and treasures, they've seen everywhere.

A flip-flop drifts by, like a mighty old ship,
Carried by currents on a daring trip.
A starfish bemoans, "Where's my leg gone awry?
I swear it was right here - oh me, oh my!"

Seagulls trade gossip beneath the blue sky,
"Did you hear what the sand said? It's all such a lie!"
While waves whisper tales that tickle the shore,
Of mermaids with parties, and ocean galore.

So dig in the sand, let secrets unfold,
With laughter and giggles more precious than gold.
The beach is a playground where jokes never cease,
With whimsy and wonder, we find our release.

The Rhythm of the Sea's Heart

The waves dance and twirl like a jolly old mate,
Telling funny tales from a sandcastle's gate.
A fish in a tux fumbles his show,
Slips on a kelp, and off he does go!

Seaweed sways gently, like a laughing friend,
"Join in the party, let's twist and pretend!"
The tide rolls in close, then out with a giggle,
As a dolphin leaps high, doing flippy-fish wiggle.

Seagulls crack jokes, flapping wings full of cheer,
"Who stole my potato chip? Oh my, oh dear!"
With laughter erupting from shells in the dusk,
The ocean does thrum, sweet and robust.

A concert of silliness, echoed in the blue,
With rhythms of joy that ripple on through.
So dance with the waves, let your worries be,
For life is a blast, down here by the sea!

Journeying through the Ocean's Veins

A crab in a tux, strutting with glee,
Says, "Look at me, I'm fancy as can be!"
A fish in a bowler hat swims right past,
"Hope you don't mind, I'm late to the bash!"

Seagulls squawk jokes, perched high on a rock,
Telling tales about a fish named Jock.
They laugh 'til they cry, 'bout a whale's new hair,
"It looked fabulous, but he's starting to share!"

Octopus juggling shells, quite the delight,
He trips on his arms, oh what a sight!
Starfish play poker, they want to be seen,
"I fold, I fold! I'm just part of the scene!"

So join in the fun, splash into the sea,
Where laughter's the current, and it's always free!
With a wink and a wave, the day feels so right,
In this wild underwater, whimsical night!

Waves of Memory

A dolphin once dreamt he could fly in the air,
He jumped through a hoop, with a stylish flair.
But alas, he fell flat, the seaweed his bed,
"Next time," he sighed, "I'll just stick to my spread!"

Old seashells whisper tales so absurd,
Of a fish with a mustache who fancied a bird.
They danced on the waves, made quite the scene,
But the bird just squawked, "You're totally green!"

A lobster with dreams of being a chef,
Opened a diner with a large sea kelp ref.
But crabs stole his apron, his hat, and his tools,
"Guess I'll be dining on seaweed for fools!"

So treasure these laughs, they float in the foam,
In the vastness of blue, they'll always find home.
For memories collide like a laugh on the shore,
In the laughter-filled waves, there's always room for more!

Currents of Existence

In the depths of the blue, where the fish fall in line,
They practice their dance, oh so perfectly fine.
But one little guppy tripped over a rock,
And created a whirlpool, now that's quite a shock!

A sardine parade, all shiny and sleek,
They honk and they giggle, playing hide-and-seek.
But one sneaky shrimp is plotting his scheme,
To crash the event and join in the dream!

A whale with a ukulele strums out a tune,
He serenades crabs under the glowing moon.
They tap their big claws, in perfect time,
Singing out loud, "Oh, we've got some prime!"

So dive into fun, let your worries subside,
In this world beneath waves, take it in stride.
For the currents of life are a magical show,
Laughter, my friend, is the best way to flow!

Whispers of the Deep

Down in the depths where the sea cucumbers chill,
A clam quips, "I'm not ready for that fishing thrill!"
With pearls in their ears, they start to debate,
"Is it real, is it fake, or just fashionable bait?"

An eel tells a story, quite tall and absurd,
Of a turtle who danced with a wonderful bird.
They twirled in the deep, quite the sight to behold,
Till a wave whisked them off, not quite as they told!

Sandy the starfish plays jokes on the shore,
"I'm five-pointed, get it? Can you handle more?"
But the sea urchins roll their eyes, they all know,
That humor is best when you're part of the show!

So listen and laugh in the sea's grand ballet,
Each whisper holds secrets in a splashing display.
For in every tidal twist, there's a joke to be found,
In the whispers of deep, laughter surely abounds!

Dance of the Salty Breeze

The seagulls are dancing, with wings in a flap,
They spin and they twist, nearly lose their map.
"Hey mate! Watch me dive!" one shouts, full of cheer,
But only finds lunch when he lands on a pier!

A crab in the sand moves with rhythm and flair,
"Come join the conga! There's music out there!"
The clams and the mussels all follow the beat,
Throwing seaweed confetti down by their feet!

A starfish on saxophone plays with such class,
While dolphins do jazz, flipping high in the mass.
"Let's groove like the waves, feel the oceanic ease,
In the dance of the salty, wind-blown breeze!"

So join in the frolic, don't let it pass us,
The ocean is a party, full of joyous ruckus.
With laughter and movement, a splash of delight,
In this dance of the salty, the world feels just right!

Journey Through Liquid Eternity

Waves giggle as they crash and roll,
Splash like laughter, tickling the shoal.
Fish play tag in their watery game,
While crabs do the cha-cha, oh what a fame!

Seagulls caw with a sarcastic flair,
As dolphins dance without a care.
Surfboards glide on this playful foam,
Who knew the ocean felt so much like home?

Shells whisper secrets of comical schemes,
Eels tease the fish with silly dreams.
Coral reefs chuckle with colors so bright,
In this liquid playground, joy takes flight!

So raise your glass to the splashy delight,
Where every splash feels just so right.
Under the sun's warm, cheeky watch,
Join in the fun, let's all just swatch!

Shadows Cast by Turquoise Skies

Bubbles rise, making the sea look silly,
While shadows dance, oh what a frilly!
Octopi hiding, playing peek-a-boo,
Wiggly things making faces, who knew?

Starfish stuck, with a grin on their face,
Dreaming of races in their own slow pace.
Sea turtles glide with a graceful twist,
"Catch me if you can!" they smugly persist.

Jellyfish float with their jelly-like jig,
Wobbling softly, looking so big.
Waves toss us about in a flurry of fun,
While we laugh and scream under the sun!

Life's a big circus in this saltwater realm,
With each splash and giggle, we take the helm.
So let's ride the waves till the day is done,
With shadows in turquoise, we've already won!

Symphony of the Submerged

Whales sing songs that tickle the ear,
Their melodies echo, spreading good cheer.
Crabs beat their claws to a whimsical tune,
As the ocean sways beneath the bright moon.

Anemones dance in a colorful trance,
While fish scurry past in their best little prance.
Shells clink together, making a beat,
Creating a symphony at the ocean's feet.

Clownfish giggle, full of delight,
Making jokes in the soft, setting light.
The seafloor sways to the rhythm they share,
In this underwater fair, life's beyond compare!

So let's toast to the music deep down below,
Where the strange and the funny put on a show!
With each joyful wave, we join in the cheer,
A symphony of laughter we hold dear!

The Wind's Embrace on Ocean Breath

The wind plays tricks, blowing hats from our heads,
While seagulls dive down, making raucous spreads.
Sand tickles our toes, oh, how we squeal,
As waves crash and roar, telling us how they feel!

On surfboards we wobble, the ocean's wild ride,
As fish flip and flop, with laughter as their guide.
The breeze wraps around us, a feather-light hug,
While seaweed does the twist, what a wriggly bug!

Sunshine drapes over, gleaming like gold,
While waves whisper stories that are funny and bold.
As crabs march in dance, all in a line,
We chuckle along, feeling quite divine!

So let out a giggle as the sea breezes blow,
In the embrace of the waves, it's a circus show!
With laughter and fun floating high in the air,
Join this frolicking saga, if you dare!

Celestial Embrace of the Coral

In a party down below, fish wear their best,
A crab with a hat thinks he's the guest.
Starfish dance, they've got no shame,
While a grouper shimmies, trying to play the game.

An octopus winks, he's a slippery fellow,
With ink like confetti, he makes quite the jello.
A clam sings loudly, though it's quite off-key,
But the seaweed just sways, grooving with glee.

A treasure chest gossips with a sunken shoe,
Making fun of the starfish, 'What's up with you?'
Jellyfish jiggle, with no sense of space,
While sea cucumbers just slow down the pace.

So here's to the coral, with friends quite absurd,
In this underwater world, you'll never feel blurred.
Life's a big party, no reason to pout,
Just watch where you step, or you'll end up a sprout!

Luminescent Shadows

In the moonlit surf, shadows play tricks,
A dolphin snickers, 'What's up with those flicks?'
The sea cucumbers, all lined in a row,
Say, 'Keep it down, we just want to glow!'

A flashlight fish beams, but it blinks way too fast,
Sardines school together, hoping this phase won't last.
Glowworms giggle, lighting the dark,
They lure in the fishes, but miss the mark.

The whispers of the waves, so playful and light,
Hold secrets of laughter, deep into the night.
A stingray slides by, trying to dance,
Just ends up flopping, but gives it a chance.

The ocean's a circus, a colorful show,
With friends made of bubbles who put on a glow.
So let's raise a fin, to this whimsical quest,
In the depths of the sea, we're all here for jest!

The Ocean's Lament

Oh, the waves complain, they spill all the tea,
'I lost my cool, I'm just an old sea!'
A whale blows a bubble, it floats up so far,
'Trying to reach land, but I just hit a bar!'

Octopuses sigh with a heavy old heart,
Recollecting the days they were good at their art.
They used to be painters with ink swirls so fine,
But now they just scribble, it's hard to define.

Anemones grumble, 'We're stuck in a tide,'
While seahorses quip, 'But at least we've got pride!'
Sand dollars whisper 'Is it all just a game?'
While barnacles chuckle, 'Hey, we're all the same!'

But laughter erupts as the tide rolls in,
'Let's dance through our troubles, and take it on the chin!'

So here's a toast to the woes of the sea,
We're all just afloat, so just let us be!

Siren's Call Unheard

In the depths a siren sings, sweet and bizarre,
But fishermen laugh, 'Aren't you a star?'
Her voice is lovely, but they just can't hear,
So she switches to hiccups, spreads laughter and cheer.

With scales that shimmer, she's quite the sight,
Pelicans squawk, 'Aren't you out at night?'
She waves a fin, and they roll their eyes,
'Sing us a song that doesn't frighten the flies!'

Seagulls join in, trying to match her claim,
All of them flapping, no one's quite the same.
The siren just shrugs, and pulls out her flute,
A kazoo from a clam makes this party astute!

The ocean erupts with a burst of delight,
As creatures unite in a whimsical fight.
So here's to the sirens, both funny and bold,
In the grand scheme of waves, laughter never gets old!

www.ingramcontent.com/pod-product-compliance
Lightning Source LLC
Chambersburg PA
CBHW060145230426
43661CB00003B/577